The Story of
Saint Patrick

by
J. Janda

illustrated by
Christopher Fay

PAULIST PRESS
New York/Mahwah, NJ

Dedication

For Marge Scanlon, her daughter,
Deidre, and grandsons,
Joseph Patrick, Stephen Francis, and
Peter Peter Pumpkin Eater

Acknowledgment

The "Deer's Cry," rewritten by the author,
is from
The Knights of God
by Patricia Lynch
London; The Bodley Head, 1969

Cover design by Moe Berman.
Cover Illustration by Christopher Fay.

Janda, J. (James), 1936-
    The story of Saint Patrick / by James A. Janda : illustrated by Christopher Fay.
        p.   cm.
    ISBN 0-8091-6623-2 (pbk.)
    1. Patrick, Saint, 373?-463?—Juvenile literature. 2. Christian saints—Ireland—Biography—Juvenile literature. [1. Patrick, Saint, 373?-463? 2. Saints.] I. Title.
BR1720.P26J36   1994
270.2´092—dc20
[B}
                                                            94-22992
                                                               CIP
                                                                AC

Published by Paulist Press
997 Macarthur Boulevard
Mahwah, New Jersey 07430

Printed and bound in the
United States of America

•▾•▴1. Patrick's Early Years▴•▾•

A little boy liked to sit on a hill and watch the boats come and go in and out of the harbor. His name was Patrick.

He liked to run down to the pier. He liked to watch the fishermen bring in their boats loaded with fish.

Patrick lived on the shore of England facing the Irish Sea. He wore a toga and sandals, because he was a citizen of Rome. He lived there a very long time ago—in the fifth century.

Patrick had to learn his prayers just as you and I. But, to tell the truth, young Patrick was more interested in playing

than in learning. He liked to climb trees, pick apples, and play with his dog.

Patrick had a happy time until he turned sixteen. Then something happened that made him very sad.

From the top of the hill, he saw it all coming. Nial, the Celtic warrior, and his enemy boats were coming into the harbor.

Nial's warriors attacked the town. They killed many people. They burned the homes. They stole horses, pigs, and

sheep. They captured Patrick, forced him into a boat, and sailed across the sea to Ireland. In Ireland, Patrick was sold as a slave.

•▼•▲2. Patrick the Slave▲•▼•

Patrick had to live in a hut and watch the sheep. He missed his family and friends. He had no one to turn to. It was in his sadness that Patrick started to pray. He began talking to God and God listened.

He always felt better after he prayed. Then he would run with his sheepdog. He would feel thankful for his old master who gave him milk, bread, and cheese to eat.

•▼•▲3. Patrick the Dreamer▲•▼•

Patrick was kept as a slave in Ireland for six years. Toward the end of his sixth year (when he was twenty-two years old), he began having dreams. These dreams he never forgot, because each of these dreams came true.

One night, Patrick dreamed that he would soon leave Ireland. As you will see, this dream came true.

The next night, he dreamed that there was a boat in the harbor to take him back home to his family and friends. When he woke, he ran to the harbor. There was the boat to carry him home!

•▼•▲4. Back Home in England▲•▼•

When his family and friends saw him, they welcomed him with open arms. They begged him never to leave them again.

He stayed with them and was very happy, but then he had another dream, a dream that changed his life.

In this dream, he saw a man named Victor. Victor gave him a pack of letters. They were from the Irish begging him to return. Then he heard many people calling to him. They were standing on the shore begging him to return to Ireland—

to live with them. They were shouting, "Come live with us and walk with us again."

Patrick woke. Then he remembered all the good people in Ireland. He remembered the songs they sang. He remembered the food they shared with him. He remembered the sheep he cared for—and his dog. Yes, he missed them all.

But he also dreamed he wanted to be a priest. He wanted to bring the peace of Christ to the Irish. He knew what he had to do.

Patrick studied. He learned how to say mass, to visit the sick, and bless the dying.

And years later, these dreams came true. He took a boat to Ireland. He left England as a priest, as a bishop.

•▾•▴5. Back in Ireland▴•▾•

Before Patrick could tell the Irish about Christ's message of peace, he knew he had to see the king. His name was Laoghaire. Patrick needed the king's permission to tell others about Christ. And so he slowly followed the road to the Hill of Tara where the king lived.

•▾••▲6. Benen▲•▾•

On the way, a man named Segne welcomed Patrick to his cottage for food, rest, and sleep. As it was getting dark, and because Patrick was tired, he agreed.

Segne had a son. His name was Benen. When Benen saw Patrick, he took a liking to him. Benen had learned to play the harp, and so, while Patrick ate with his father, Benen played his harp for them.

The next morning, as Patrick was about to leave, Benen grabbed Patrick's leg and sat on his shoe. He did not want Patrick to leave. He would not move. Only after his father asked Patrick if Benen could go along with him—and Patrick agreed—did Benen get off his shoe.

So Benen left with Patrick to see the king.

•▼•▲7. On the Way to Tara Hill▲•▼•

On the road, Patrick saw six men.

"Where are you going?" they asked.

"To see the king," answered Patrick. "I want to bring him Christ's message of peace."

"Can we come along?" they asked. "We have enough food for you and your little friend."

"Come, join us. You are welcome," said Patrick.

As they walked, he explained to them all about Christ's message of peace. It was growing dark when they reached the Hill of Slane. As it was the night before Easter Sunday, the day Christians celebrate Christ's rising from the dead, they stopped and made camp.

After all had eaten their fill, Patrick lit the Easter fire and they all prayed and sang aloud, "Christ Our Light."

•▼•▲8. King Laoghaire▲•▼•

From the Hill of Tara, miles away, King Laoghaire saw the fire in the distant darkness. Across the plain of Meath, he

watched the fire burning. Lochru, his chief Druid, seeing the fire, shouted, "Whoever lit that fire must die. It is against the law to light a fire during these sacred days."

Laoghaire immediately called his warriors. Then, joined by the Druids, they all leapt to their horses and rode to the Hill of Slane to punish the offenders.

•▼•▲9. Patrick Prepares to▲•▼• Meet the King

Benen was the first to hear the thunder of hooves off in the distance. "Horses," he said. They all were afraid. Patrick saw the fear in their eyes. He got up and said, "Let us call on the angels to guide and protect us."

Then he began to pray.

"I buckle to my heart
This day,

Christ's angels to
Protect the way,

With shields of light
And power bright,

To cheer and guard
Me on the way."

•▾•▲10. Patrick Meets the King▲•▾•

Then Patrick said, "Wait here. I will go alone. Let us see whose weapons are more powerful—the angels' shield of light or weapons made to hurt and harm." And off he walked alone in the wind and rain. This time, even Benen was too frightened to argue with him.

When Laoghaire and his band saw him coming, they reined their horses. "Who are you, and why have you come?" shouted Lochru.

"I am Patrick. I have come in peace. I only wish to see the king to tell him of Christ—Christ Our Light."

"So you lit that fire?" snarled Lochru.

"Yes," said Patrick.

Lochru and his Druids jumped from their horses to kill Patrick, but they could not approach him. Something held them back. It was as if an invisible shield kept them from approaching him. They grabbed their daggers and struck only the wind.

When Laoghaire saw this, he was amazed. The Druids could not come near Patrick, but kept stabbing the wind.

Laoghaire started to laugh. His Druids looked comical. "Enough," he shouted. "Patrick, tomorrow you are welcome to the halls of Tara. I wish to hear more of 'Christ Our Light.'" Then to Lochru and the Druids he barked, "Stop. Patrick is welcome to my halls."

Lochru and the Druids did as they were told. They slowly mounted their horses, but they were confused. The ride back to Tara, though, cleared their heads. They grew angry when they realized that they had appeared like fools.

•▼••▲11. Lochru Plans to▲•▼• Kill Patrick

When at last they were inside the walls of Tara, Lochru met with his Druids in private. "This man, Patrick, must die. Tomorrow we will secretly leave for the crossroad very early in the morning. We will hide ourselves, and when he and his band cross there, we shall rush up and kill them."

●▼●▲12. Patrick Returns to Camp▲●▼●

Patrick, meanwhile, had walked back to his friends in hiding. When he saw them, he shouted, "Christ rules, Christ reigns, Christ conquers—with only love." Then he began to laugh. "Tomorrow, we see the High King, Laoghaire, at Tara Hill."

And so it was. The next morning found Patrick and his friends on the road to Tara Hill. As they walked, Patrick talked. Again he saw the fear in their eyes for none of them carried weapons. And

yes, Benen was huddled between them. They had promised to live by Christ's teachings to harm no living thing, but their minds were filled with fear.

"Our power, our strength," began Patrick, "is the power of Christ in our hearts. It can do so much more than we can ask or imagine. Did not Christ promise in the Holy Books that the powers of darkness cannot prevail? Join me in song. Let us sing of Christ." Then they all joined Patrick and sang:

> "Christ at my right hand,
> Christ at my left hand;
>
> Christ in front of me,
> Christ behind me;
>
> Christ above me,
> Christ below me;
>
> Christ within me,
> Christ outside of me;
>
> Christ everywhere,
> Everywhere Christ."

●▼●▲14. The Deer's Cry▲●▼●

They continued singing as they passed through the crossroad with Benen trailing at the end with his bundle and harp—following the road to Tara Hill to see the king. They did not notice

Lochru and his band in hiding, nor did Lochru and his band notice them. All Lochru and his band noticed was a small herd of deer pass over the crossroad—followed by a fawn.

The Druids were growing bored and restless, hiding and waiting near the crossroad, waiting to kill Patrick and his friends. "Lochru," one of them finally said, "this Patrick and his band must have had a change of heart. They are running from us like dogs with their tails between their legs, back to Britain where they came from." Then he came out of hiding and walked up and down the crossroad. "See," he said, "the roads are empty. Not a soul in sight. Come, see for yourself."

Then they all came out of hiding, because they knew that Lochru felt so much hate in his heart, he did not know what he was doing. Lochru finally came out, too, looked in all four directions—up and down the crossroad—but saw nothing.

"Back to Tara Hill," he snapped. He knew that in some strange way, he had been defeated, and he was in a very bad mood.

"The day is not wasted," joked one of the Druids. "We did see a stag leading his band of deer at the crossroad. A fawn was following them."

"But that was hours ago," said another.

"I know," said Lochru who had heard the deer singing. "I don't like this," he muttered as he followed the Druids back to Tara Hill. "On the fawn's back was a bundle and a harp," he added, but none of them heard him.

To this day, the song that Patrick and his friends sang as they passed by Lochru and his band is known as "The Deer's Cry."

•▾•▲15. Cead Mile Failte▲•▾•

Meanwhile, Patrick and his friends were being welcomed by the warriors and poets in the hall of the High King. And there at the far end of the hall stood Laoghaire himself who shouted, "Cead mile failte," that is, "a hundred thousand welcomes." His beautiful queen, Angus, stood beside him.

Patrick and his friends approached the king and bowed low.

"Tell us, Patrick, tell us about your God, Christ Our Light."

Patrick paused a few seconds before he addressed the king.

"I know you wish peace in your lands, O king. Buckle to your heart this day the power of Christ. This is the power that unites, the power that respects. It guides, it guards, it protects. It is the power of love.

"This is our teaching: Do unto others as you would have them do unto you. Forgive those who harm you, just as your Father in heaven forgives you."

Patrick then went on to tell all about the life of Christ. All listened. Then he paused and spoke the following words:

"This is the message I wish to spread throughout your kingdom. I wish all your people to live in Christ's peace, harmony, and light."

King Laoghaire sat spellbound. Patrick's words were like music to his ears. Yes, the words of Patrick had

touched his heart. Tears were streaming
down Queen Angus' cheeks.

Slowly the king arose and spoke, "I
shall consider all you have said."

Then he heard Lochru and his Druids entering the high hall.

With a loud voice that all could hear, he announced, "Let all know that Patrick has my protection and consent to spread the message of Christ, his God, throughout my kingdom. Whoever harms Patrick, harms me."

Patrick's heart swelled with joy hearing the words of the king. Then with his face shining like the sun, with a firm voice, he sang,

"I buckle to my heart
This day,

The love of God
To show the way,

His eye to watch,
His ear to hear,

His hand to lead
Me on the way."

•▾•▲16. The Final Years▲•▾•

Patrick spent the rest of his life living his dream, telling anyone and everyone about Christ and his message of peace and forgiveness. Yes, for Patrick the dreamer, all of his dreams came true.

Not all would listen and believe. Some chose to give hatred a home in their hearts. When this happened, he would forgive them, those who chose violence, not peace, for truly he had the power of the Father above, Christ at his side, and the Spirit in his heart.

The Father above, Christ at our side, and the Spirit in our hearts—three Persons in one God—One in Three. When the Irish asked, "How can that be?"— Patrick showed them the shamrock, the three-leaved clover. "See," he said, "the clover has three leaves, but it is one. This is the mystery of the Holy Trinity—Three in One, One in Three." And that is why people wear shamrocks on Saint Patrick's Day.

After a full life, Patrick died with Benen at his side. Benen, who was then a priest, later became bishop to carry on the work Patrick had begun.

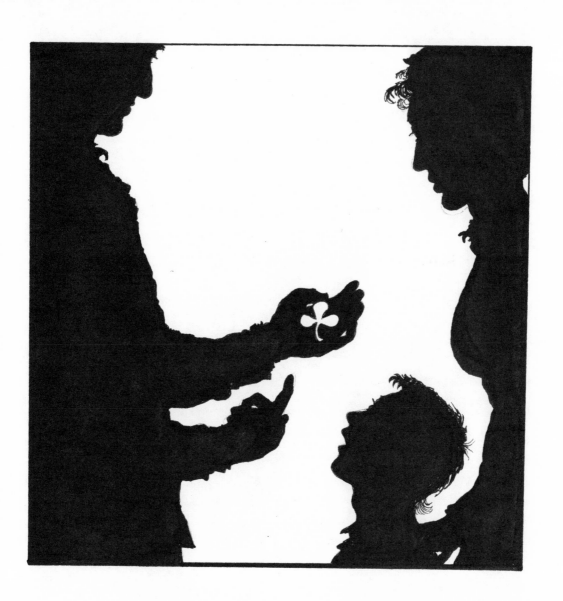